Lesson Plans

Brandon Thornton

BookLeaf Publishing

India | USA | UK

Presentation by *BookLeaf Publishing*

Web: www.bookleafpub.com

E-mail: info@bookleafpub.com

ISBN: 9789360943868

First edition 2024

*This book is dedicated to the love of my life,
my dog, Rocky.*

ACKNOWLEDGEMENT

I am extremely grateful for every student that's ever entered my classroom, school, and world, as well as my teachers -- past, present, and future. You all inspire me more than any stanza can capture.

PREFACE

Being Black has had its difficulties. Being gay has had its difficulties as well, but teaching is the most difficult aspect of my life. If that's true for you, then maybe these pages will bring you peace.

Problems

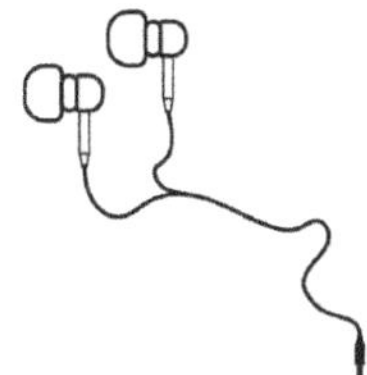

As you play on your phone, I encourage you to
consider the problems.
No, I don't mean the untouched problems on this
in-class activity.
I mean the real problems.
Because when you go home,
your parents are going to ask
about those problems.
You're going to tell them that you're having
problems focusing in class.
Your parents are going to reach out to me
around bedtime — disregarding my problems.
Now, we've all got problems.
And you?
You've got Snapchat.
While everyone around you problem-solves

on what THEY can be doing better to
help you through these problems.
Rinse, repeat, resign or retire.
Do you see the problems here?

Microaggression

Lemme get this straight.
That because I get my hair cut at Great
Clips…I'm WHITE?
Even though we all came here on great ships
Spent months inside moms, stretched out their
hips
But shhh…I should watch these big lips.
Because big lips have big words…
and behind these big words are big hands
and behind these hands are NOT "deez nuts" but
140 characters waiting to be used…
To hurt.
To judge.
To make you feel every ounce of uncertainty I
feel when YOU say:
"You're not really black."

Overalls

Oh.
Hey there.
I saw you AGAIN today.
You had on a polka dot button up and (surprise),
overalls.
And overall, I was pretty damn pissed.
Pissed that, overall, you still seemed pretty damn
happy.
Overall, I'd say that this makes me pretty damn
petty —
But, to me, petty is wearing overalls with a smile
that says,
overall,
you're doing just fine without me.
Over ALL the things I can't un-see today,
you and your hipster overalls top the list.

Stress Eating, Quietly

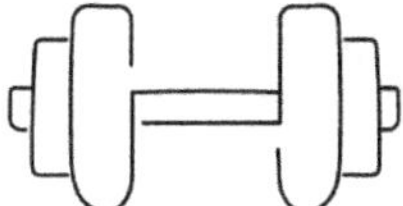

He pulls the body of his friend out from
beneath the depths of his bathroom sink,
Quietly.

He steps onto his face and his friend screams.
His friend screams two-hundred and four
reasons to get off.
He does,
Quietly.

He then pulls into Gold's Gym and finds the
quietest corner
to match the quietest aisle he just visited at
Wal-Mart.
But, these people are practically perfect.
These people aren't like him.

So, he hits the road at the quietest times
and runs along the quietest parts of the trail.
People pass him and some even wave,

Quietly.

After a week, he pays his friend a visit once
more.
But this time, his friend only offers
two-hundred reasons to leave him alone.
And he does,
Quietly.

He pushes and pushes and, quietly, pulls his
hamstring.

And now he sits in his room, quietly –
eating the super-size portion of food to match
the super-size portion of disappointment.

And he wonders….
if obesity is such a loud problem in America,
then why is everything around him so…

quiet.

Finstas

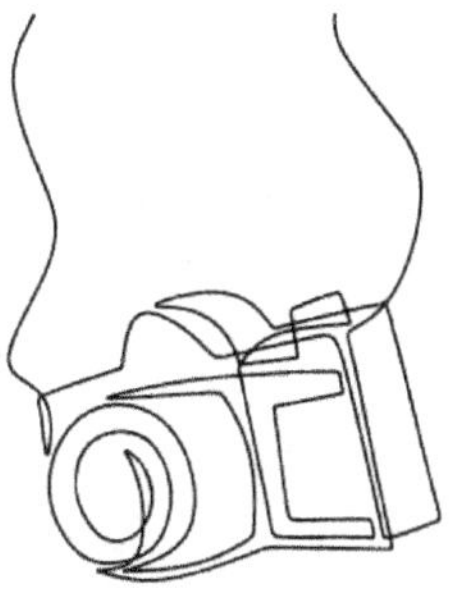

In the end, he did it for the likes.
He craned his neck, stretched his arm
until he heard the snap, crackle, pop of the
camera —

Cheese Louise.

Instead of saying what he meant to say
he stretched his 150 characters into word play.
You'd think with his education he'd be able to
stretch his mind.

But no, he did it for the likes.
And still…people flocked to his pages.
Perhaps to watch the rise of an icon
or perhaps to watch his descent into vanity.

I guess they needed company.

Likely.
Like me.

Because I wrote this for you.

And in the end, I did it for the likes.

LOL

And then he said, "I almost turned off my body cam."

I did an inaudible gasp at the lack of gasps from those around us.
I did a double take at the empty plates and full faces of glee.
I did some reflection on how I found myself here — the token black guy.

Again.

It's funny because that wasn't a joke. It was a story.
It's funny because I laughed to hide my discomfort.
It's funny because if it were in an iMessage I'd respond with "lol" and get on with my life.

It's funny because an unarmed black boy had
been shot that weekend.
It's funny because this bbq was to commemorate
our independence...yet I still wear chains.

Naw...the joke is on them.

Because massa taught me how to write.
And all. my. life. I's. had. to. fight.

Isn't that funny?

On This Day

Facebook.
Why?
I made it a point to not block my ex
because that much effort would show that I care.
I don't care…
that much.

But your flashbacks to how happy we were
usually leads me down the path of how happy he
currently is.
I don't care…
that much.

But if you were able to manipulate fake news
then surely you're able to sense the dread in my
search history,
the tone in my statuses,
and the lack of a new profile pic after 2012.
Why not send me videos of my ALS challenge?

Those were happier days.

Again, I don't care...that much.
I just thought I had the strength to finally hit the
"block" button.
But then I noticed that you added a new option.
Above "unfollow" it now says "take a break".

It's funny. Because that was once an option for
us.
And now I'm just looking to break back into the
dating scene.

Except I'm not.

Because broken pieces don't always get put back
together.
They just get swept aside, waiting to cut the next
person who reaches out.

Are You Still Watching?

Netflix does this thing where they change the
artwork for their titles.
They catch my eye every time.

My heart skips a beat at the idea of a new
obsession
— and then it slows at the realization that
… I've been here before.

So I keep scrolling, looking for the next
disappointment.
The screen fades to black momentarily and I
catch my reflection.
Whoop there it is.

It Wasn't Lit

"Hey bro, is that an IPA?"

I chuckled at the question
as I clutched my seltzer with both hands.
You see the last bar had beer for $12 a can
and the math teacher in me said,
I think I can, I think I can not
wait until the next bar.

We went from a dimly lit rooftop bar
to a college lit basement bar.
And I'm not talking Shakespeare
Although it was poetic when he finished his
question:
"We don't sip our beer with two hands, brother."

The smile faded.

Just when I thought I was home,
here I was a Montague at a bar full of Capulets.

Suddenly the music felt less lit and more
dodgeball.
There I stood.
Awkwardly waiting to get picked last to get hit
on and outed first.
I grabbed my phone and quickly swiped up to
close Grindr,
which also feels a lot like dodgeball sometimes.
Tonight was no exception.

Although I had hoped that my new friend would
make an exception.
Maybe this one time he would see black and
queer as coexisting.
And maybe this one time he could see the label
on my beer as unrelated
to the labels I wore when I entered this bar.
The same labels that now how had scratch marks
at the corner where I tried to peel them.

Luckily, the bell rang to "Like a Virgin".
You would think that the music would give me
enough
strength to wave bye as I swallowed the lyrics. It
didn't.

Instead, I traded in my rainbow flag for a white
one and nodded
in the most black, masculine way I could think --
a nod to conformity.

Anime Club

Anime trends on every spirit week.
Anime ends a popular streak,
unless you're already popular.

Then it's cool.

And I may scream,
because this anime life is not for the weak.

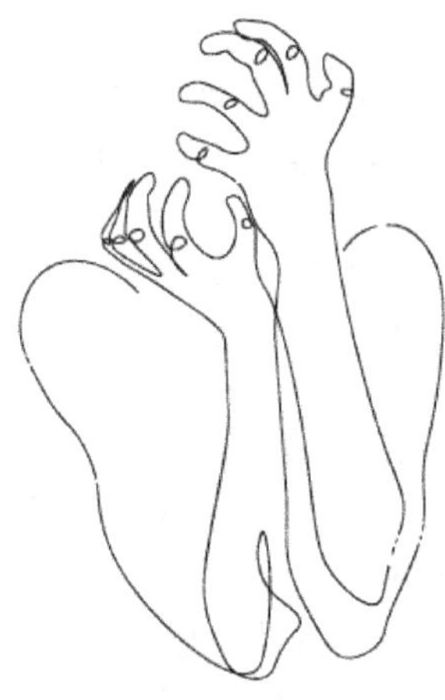

Life, Liberty, and the Pursuit

I was on my favorite song when I noticed you
walking by.
I don't know if this is unique to being a Black
male (it is) —
but for me there is always a dilemma.

Do I wave to make you feel safe or do I avoid
eye contact to make you feel safe?

Today, like every other day and every couple of
footsteps, I made a choice.

You see, I was feeling great.
I was feeling the lyrics of my favorite music
spreading over me,
my weight loss goals slowly making progress,
and the simultaneous relief and exhaustion of
students pulling up their grades.

So, I took a leap of faith and pulled up my head
and hand to wave —
a signal of solidarity —
that we're both out here
chasing life, liberty, and the pursuit of happiness
on constitution trail —

or at the very least — health and sunshine.

But…the way you clutched onto your purse,
the way you tucked it under your arm and then
moved it to your other side,
and the way your eyes shot daggers that pierced
my posture and soul as you sped up,
helped me understand the phrase, "if looks could
kill."

And the handful of others who continued to
follow suit.…
their eyes told me more than I needed to feel
today.

You.

You don't know me.
You just think you do.
You were never in danger of being robbed,
and you have absolutely nothing I could ever
want…

except the freedom to exist,
to matter.

And the freedom to run FROM my problems
not alongside them.

Recess

I have found that the best place to hide my
thoughts is in my words.

Not in the books that I read or the stanzas I write
but the words…

The words that I bite as I chew on the yes.
Cuz it's nice to feel wanted and yes I never
wanted
to play hide and seek —
cuz arts and crafts were more of my jam.

And by jam I mean beats, K-Pop, and Bach
while I eat, crafting words that show that I'm not

Depressed,

stressed,
And less than the me
I dreamed, I screamed, I knew I would be….
by now.

So I cover my eyes with your likes, reacts,
your snaps and your crap that cleverly deny
the real me
that seeks the fake you.

And the moment I do,
I yell olly, olly, oxen free —
because I can't make time for me,
while socially promoting B
when I have to be, professionally —T.

It's almost poetic.

And pathetic how you can be surrounded by
love and shivering with loneliness.

Yes.

These ideas are not mutually exclusive —
And someday I'd like to be somewhat exclusive

But, 3…2…1. Time.

Ready or not? Here I come!

Microagression (Revisited)

Today one of my favorite students reminded me
AGAIN that I'm "not really black."

And I admit, this time it stings.

It stings that he believes that our blackness is a
choice.

It stings that at 15 he believes blackness and
education to be mutually exclusive.

But, most of all, it stings that — at 15 — I
viewed those words as a compliment…wore
them like a badge,

a get out of jail free card,

a VIP pass.

Because what else do you do when someone proudly proclaims that you do not exist?

But I know too much now.

I know that we are just as essential as bees,

just as desired…

yet, just as endangered.

And I admit, that stings too.

But not as much as the whips, rocks, and stares those before me had to endure for me to be able to write this now, for me to be able to teach him tomorrow, and for him to be able to hold that basketball I proudly watch him shoot.

And…yeah, I know that us bees should stick together…

But right now, I hope he's reading this.

And I hope it stings.

Just Another Drill

Today, another one happened.
But today feels scarier…and I think you feel the
same.
You've come to the same realization
that school shootings have become a part of the
school culture.
There's no running from that fact now.
In fact, you probably have a lock-down drill
scheduled sometime in the spring.

What went wrong?

Maybe you want to talk about that.

But, truthfully, you know you don't even have
time.

Because in 12 hours you'll be in front of your
students again.
And right now, you're probably putting your
own children to bed.

You don't have the luxury of being angry,
confused, sad, or even numb.
Instead, you will need to model compassion,
understanding, love,
and most importantly, peace…

while everyone around you fights.

I hate it here...

is a joke.
It's a meme.
Hyperbole...
until it's not.

PEMDAS

Sometimes,
when I've lost complete order of the classroom,
I like to sit in silence.

If it's really bad,
I start moving desks
to pretend I'm in control again.

I've moved a lot of desks lately,
because I don't have the answers.
I
just
have
problems.

The American Dream

If you work hard,
you too can live paycheck to paycheck,
while everyone around you reminds you of your
summers off,
your glorified babysitting
and your "why"
when you ask why
you're living paycheck to paycheck
after working so hard.

Non-Mutually Exclusive

A box of chocolates contains seven milk
chocolates
and seven dark chocolates.
Three of the milk chocolates
and two of the dark chocolates have peanuts
inside.

You randomly select and eat a chocolate.

In order to find the probability of the chocolate
being a dark chocolate
or having no peanuts inside,
we must first consider:
are these two events mutually exclusive
or non-mutually exclusive.

I'll wait.

They're non-mutually exclusive.
Because the chocolate can be both dark
and have peanuts inside --

just like we can teach for the outcome
AND the income.

The School to Prison Pipeline

is a metaphor,
a dissertation,
a trend,
but it's not trendy,
and it's no longer a metaphor.

Bed

I am so sorry about all of the times I neglected
you growing up,
because now you're the one thing I can rely on,
the one thing that will cure any affliction,
the one thing that has my back.

As kids, we saw you as punishment.
But now I feel punished when I'm asked to get
out of you.

You may call this crippling depression,
And I want you to know that...
well,
you are probably onto something.

But I'm onto something too.

I'm onto bed.

Life Has Been Rocky

Some of the happiest mornings are rolling over
to you still asleep beside me.
You're actually asleep now -- all you do is sleep.
But when I come home, you are always at the
door.

Always loyal.
Always ready.
Always...Rocky.

We've been together for 17 years now
so I know our time together is short.
I'd hoped you'd be around to see me
fall in love with an actual human being,
but I spent so much time chasing degrees that
now I'm out of breath.

My chest aches at the idea of opening up again.

So instead I close it off like the doors of my five
bedroom home.
And I swipe my ID to get into work
with hopes that one day someone will swipe
right.

Ope. You're having nightmares now.

It must be nice to have them with your eyes
closed.